WONDER WOMAN

VOLUME 2 GUTS

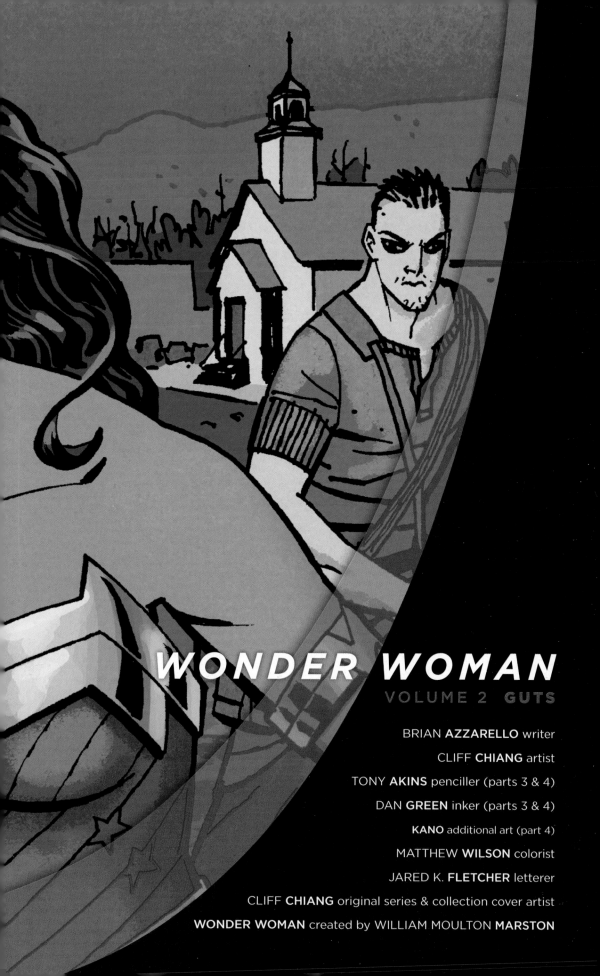

WONDER WOMAN

VOLUME 2   GUTS

BRIAN **AZZARELLO** writer

CLIFF **CHIANG** artist

TONY **AKINS** penciller (parts 3 & 4)

DAN **GREEN** inker (parts 3 & 4)

KANO additional art (part 4)

MATTHEW **WILSON** colorist

JARED K. **FLETCHER** letterer

CLIFF **CHIANG** original series & collection cover artist

WONDER WOMAN created by WILLIAM MOULTON **MARSTON**

MATT IDELSON Editor – Original Series CHRIS CONROY Associate Editor – Original Series
ROBIN WILDMAN Editor ROBBIN BROSTERMAN Design Director – Books
ROBBIE BIEDERMAN Publication Design

BOB HARRAS VP – Editor-in-Chief

DIANE NELSON President DAN DIDIO and JIM LEE Co-Publishers
GEOFF JOHNS Chief Creative Officer
JOHN ROOD Executive VP – Sales, Marketing and Business Development
AMY GENKINS Senior VP – Business and Legal Affairs NAIRI GARDINER Senior VP – Finance
JEFF BOISON VP – Publishing Operations MARK CHIARELLO VP – Art Direction and Design
JOHN CUNNINGHAM VP – Marketing TERRI CUNNINGHAM VP – Talent Relations and Services
ALISON GILL Senior VP – Manufacturing and Operations HANK KANALZ Senior VP – Digital
JAY KOGAN VP – Business and Legal Affairs, Publishing JACK MAHAN VP – Business Affairs, Talent
NICK NAPOLITANO VP – Manufacturing Administration SUE POHJA VP – Book Sales
COURTNEY SIMMONS Senior VP – Publicity BOB WAYNE Senior VP – Sales

WONDER WOMAN VOLUME 2: GUTS

DC Comics, 1700 Broadway, New York, NY 10019
A Warner Bros. Entertainment Company.
Printed by RR Donnelley, Salem, VA, USA. 12/7/12. First Printing.
HC ISBN: 978-1-4012-3809-4
SC ISBN: 978-1-4012-3810-0

Library of Congress Cataloging-in-Publication Data

Azzarello, Brian.
Wonder Woman. Volume 2, Guts / Brian Azzarello, Cliff Chiang, Tony Akins.
p. cm.
"Originally published in single magazine form in Wonder Woman 7-12."

RENZE, ITALIA.
PLEASE-- YOU DON'T UNDERSTAND...
IT'S NOT MY BUSINESS.
CLUB eros
HE WON'T LEAVE ME ALONE-- HE FOLLOWS ME EVERYWHERE...
REALLY? I DON'T SEE--
WHEN I SAW YOU TONIGHT IN THE CLUB, I TOLD HIM I HAD TO GO TO THE... HE'S OBSESSED--
NO, HE'S--
I HAVE TO HIDE FROM HIM TO GET ANY PEACE!
SO WHAT MUST I DO TO GET SOME?
MAKE HIM STOP!
STOP WHAT? WHEN WE FIRST MET, YOU WERE CRYING. I FELT PITY, SO I DID YOU A FAVOR.
BUT THESE TEARS ARE DIFFERENT, AND... NO PITY. YOU HAVE WHAT YOU WANTED.
I WAS WRONG.
IT'S NOT MY BUSINESS.
LISTEN TO ME!

I GAVE YOU WHAT YOU WANTED...
THE ONLY THING I'M INTERESTED IN HEARING IS *THANK YOU.*
LOOK, THE SUN IS COMING UP... SO, *RUN AWAY.*
WHAT YOU WANT *NOW?* IT'S NOT MY BUSINE--
EH?
WHAT'S GOING ON HERE?

A FICKLE HEART...
THAT'S NONE OF YOUR BUSINESS.
WE DO HAVE SOME.
DO "WE"?
WE NEED A FAVOR.
A FAVOR?
OF COURSE, UNCLE.

PITTING THE SEA AND HELL AGAINST HERA, THAT WAS A BAD IDEA.
SEEMED LIKE A GOOD ONE...AT THE TIME.
AH. SO IT WAS YOURS.
THE POINT OF IT WAS-- TO BLIND HERA.
MISSION ACCOMPLISHED.
TRUE, LENNOX, BUT THE COST--
--WAS SOMEONE YOU LOVED.
HER NAME IS ZOLA.
I NEED TO BRING HER BACK FROM THE SHADOWS.
THAT'S WHY WE'VE COME TO YOU, EROS.
BELLEZZA e la BESTIA
NO... YOU'VE COME TO ME BECAUSE YOU NEED SOMETHING ELSE.
THE SMITH IS A GENTLEMAN. HE DOESN'T TAKE KINDLY TO UNANNOUNCED GUESTS.
OR GUESTS IN GENERAL, MESSENGER.
DOESN'T LIKE COMPANY?

PREFERS HIS WORK.
SO DO I.
REALLY? MY MOTHER FINDS IT LACKING.
SENZA USCITA
EH? WHA'S WRONG WITH HER, THEN?
ABSOLUTELY NOTHING.
CAREFUL THERE, WONDER WOMAN...
SENZA USCITA

MOUNT ETNA.
...LOOKS CAN BE DECEIVING.

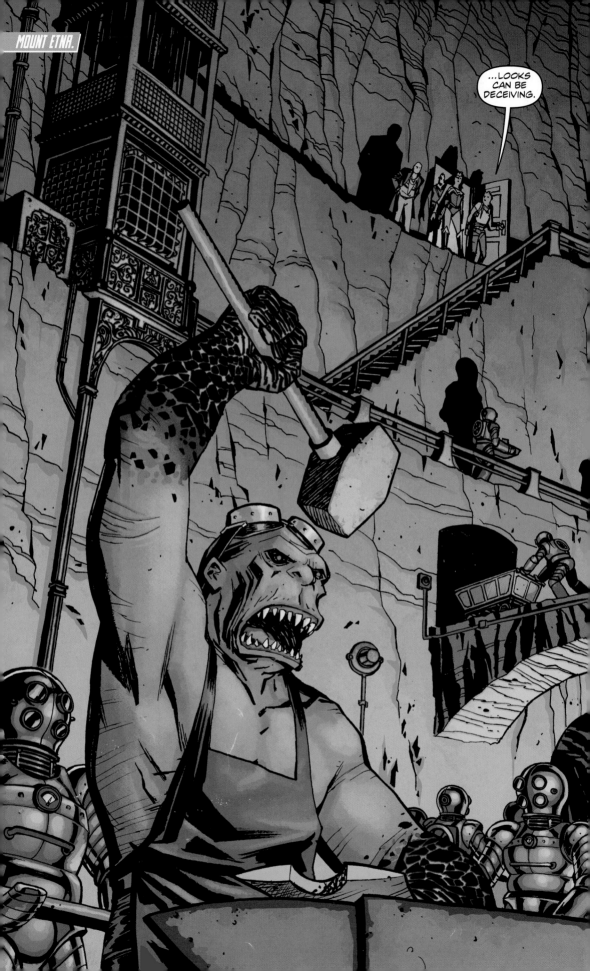

IT'LL TAKE MORE THAN WEAPONS TO BARGAIN WITH HELL.
THEY ARE A GOOD PLACE TO START, THOUGH.
MY SENTIMENTS, HEPHAESTUS. WHEN MY MOTHER GAVE ME THIS LASSO, SHE SAID YOU MADE IT.
IT'S SERVED ME WELL.
THAT? NOT A WEAPON. NOW THIS...
CRACK
THIS A WEAPON.
TAKE IT.

"SO YOU JUST LEARNED YOU'RE ZEUS' DAUGHTER, AND YOU DECIDED TO TANGLE WITH NOT JUST HIS WIFE, BUT HIS BROTHERS?
"I MUST SAY, YOU CLEARLY ARE PART OF THIS FAMILY. ALWAYS BICKERING IN ONE WAY OR ANOTHER."
IT'S SHAMEFUL.
REALLY, MESSENGER? IF I'M NOT MISTAKEN, YOU'VE BEEN CAUGHT MORE THAN ONCE--
RYYAAAAARGH

WHAT THE HELL...?
EXACTLY.
I'VE DECIDED TO ARM YOU, AND HELL IS NOT PLEASED...
SO HE'S SENT THIS ABOMINATION TO FOUL MY STUDIO!
AND I WON'T HAVE IT!
RYYYAAAA
AAARGH!

TSSSSSSS
RYYYAAAA--
HEPHAESTUS...

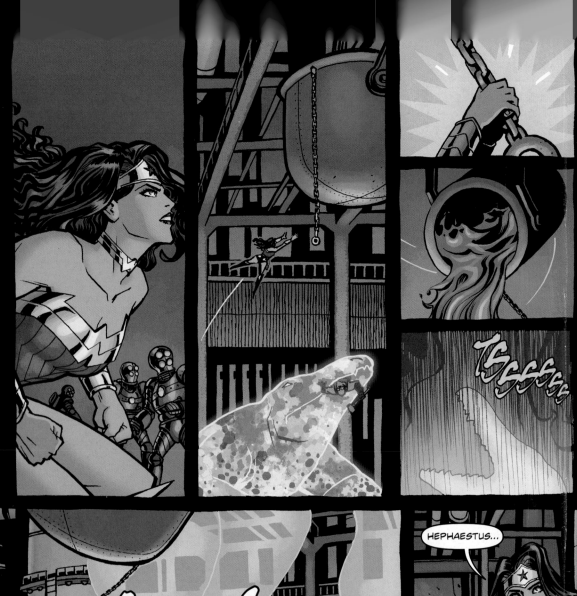

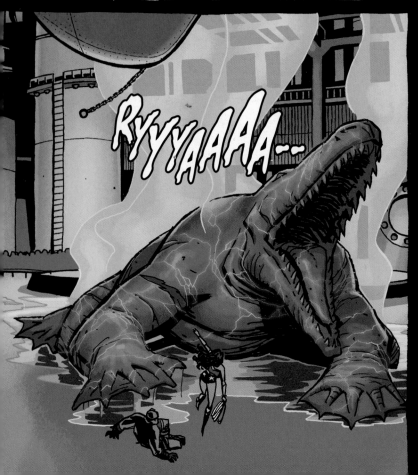

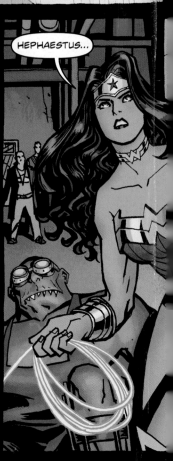

CRACK

THIS LASSO-- IN MY *HANDS*--

POINT TAKEN.

MASTER...

ALEX AND CIMON...

HMM

TIMEOS, PREPARE THEIR BODIES. THEY'LL BE COMMENDED TO THE FORGE.

WAIT...THESE AREN'T AUTOMATONS-- THINGS YOU MADE? THEY'RE *MEN*?

BROTHERS.

YOURS, ACTUALLY. ALL...

...THE MALE CHILDREN OF AMAZONS.
WHAT?
IT NEVER CROSSED YOUR MIND? HOW YOU ONLY HAVE SISTERS?
I THOUGHT IT WAS DIVINE...
HAHAHA
DIVINE? AS IN THE WILL OF THE GODS?
AS A GOD, I WILL TELL YOU THAT THEY DON'T CARE ABOUT ANYONE...
BUT THEM-SELVES.
KLANG
"WONDER WOMAN, YOUR PEOPLE, THRICE A CENTURY...

"...GO ON RAIDS. LIKE PIRATES, THEY TAKE TO THE SEA--"

FOR BOOTY.

DON'T BE CLEVER, BOY. MORTAL VESSELS ARE THEIR TARGETS--

--SEMINAL MORTAL VESSELS.

"AND THEY HAVE THEIR WAY. IT MUST SEEM LIKE A DREAM TO MOST MEN... BEAUTIFUL WOMEN, OFFERING THEMSELVES...

"BUT IT QUICKLY TURNS TO A NIGHTMARE. THEIR LIVES...

"DRAINED FROM THEM.

"TRIUMPHANT, THE AMAZONS RETURN TO PARADISE ISLAND, AND WAIT.

"NINE MONTHS LATER, SOME CELEBRATE THE BIRTH OF A DAUGHTER...

"SOME DON'T.

"SO I TRADE WEAPONS FOR FAILURES."

FOR BOYS.

YES.

TO MAN YOUR FORGE.

THAT SOUNDS LIKE AN ACCUSATION...
BETTER THAT, THAN QUESTIONING A GOD.
IS IT?
METHINKS YOU'VE GIVEN HER MUCH TO THINK ABOUT, SMITH.
HAVE I?
MIGHT'AVE HIT A DANGEROUS NERVE...
EH?
JUS' SAYIN'.
SSSSSS
A TONGUE CAN STRIKE HARDER THAN A HAMMER, AT TIMES.

AYE--
I'M AWAKE.
RIGHT. THA' MEAN--
UNFORTUNATELY? YES.
WE BOTH HAVE THE SAME IDEA.
LOOK, I AIN'T SAYIN' THAT I'M RIGHT ALL THE TIME. IN HERE, THE WIND-- SHE CAN'T SPEAK TO ME. BUT--
--THIS IS WRONG.
SLAVIN' IS WHAT IT IS.
WHA' ABOUT ZOLA?
WE CAME HERE SO WE COULD FREE HER...

"...WHY NOT SPREAD THE LOVE?"
HEPHAESTUS.
EH?
LOOKIN' FOR THIS, YEA UGLY BASTARD?
YOU SAID MY LASSO ISN'T A WEAPON, BUT WHEN ONE IS ENTWINED IN IT, THEY SPEAK THE TRUTH.
AND THAT-- THE TRUTH--IS MY WEAPON.
NO...YOUR WEAPON IS INTIMIDATION. YOU BLAME THE ROPE. THAT'S THE TRUTH.
GET--

--UP, BROTHERS!
CRASH
THAT IS A WORD I'VE NEVER USED, BUT IT BRINGS ME JOY TO USE IT...
BROTHERS!
AMAZONS...
IT IS TIME TO RISE. WE ARE WARRIORS, AND--
PLEASE, RELEASE OUR MASTER.

?
YOU ARE MAKING A HORRIBLE MISTAKE...
WE OWE THE SMITH OUR LIVES.
IF IT WASN'T FOR HIM, WE WOULD HAVE BEEN THROWN IN THE TIDE--TO DROWN, UNLOVED.
AS MY MOTHER DID TO ME... SOMETHING I COULD NEVER ALLOW.
HE WANTED US AND HE RAISED US...
HERE, WE ARE ARTISTS...
AND WE ARE HAPPY.
PLEASE... RELEASE THE MASTER.

I'M...
TIRED.
GET SOME REST. YOU'LL NEED IT.
FOR TOMORROW...
YOU CAN GO TO HELL.

CLIFF CHIANG 2011

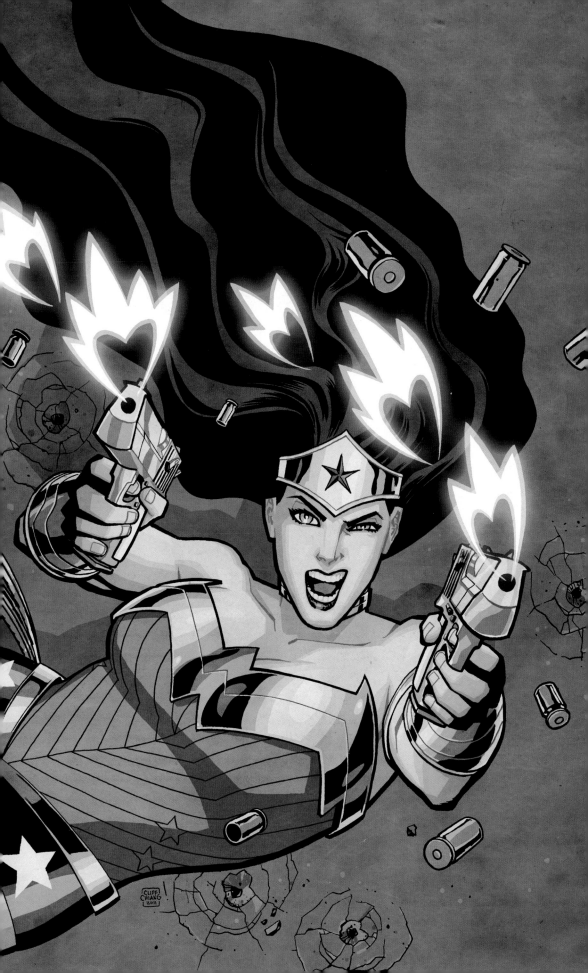

MOUNT ETNA.
THIS SEEMS PROMISING...
TAKE IT.
AS DOES THIS.
MY ARSENAL IS AT YOUR DISPOSAL.
A SHIELD, PERHAPS?
IF YOU THINK IT WILL DO SOME GOOD. THOUGH I DO FIND YOUR CHOICES...
ARCHAIC.
IT'S HOW I WAS RAISED, HEPHAESTUS.

I LIKE THE HEFT A THIS 'ERE.

YOU WON'T BE NEEDING IT, LENNOX.

I'M GOING *ALONE.*

OVER M' DEAD--

WHICH IS THE ONLY WAY IN TO THE UNDERWORLD, OTHER THAN ESCORTED BY ME.

TRUTH FROM THE MESSENGER. SURPRISING.

WE'RE READY TO GO *WITH* YOU...

≡HUMMPH≡

I KNOW, EROS. THAT'S WHY YOU CAN'T. BECAUSE IF I FAIL...

WE'LL *BE* HERE.

TAKE *THESE.*

SHE'LL BRING THEM BACK.

WHAT?!

WON'T YOU...

"...WONDER WOMAN?"
HUH.
...NOT WHAT I EXPECTED.
IT NEVER IS.
?
BUT YOU'VE BEEN HERE MANY TIMES, HERMES.
TRUE. YET EACH TIME, IT'S DIFFERENT.
THE UNDERWORLD IS GOVERNED BY HADES' WHIMS AND IMAGINATION. AS *THEY* CHANGE, SO DOES HIS REALM.
AND WHILE IT'S NOT WHAT YOU WERE EXPECTING...

...CLEARLY, HE'S EXPECTING YOU.

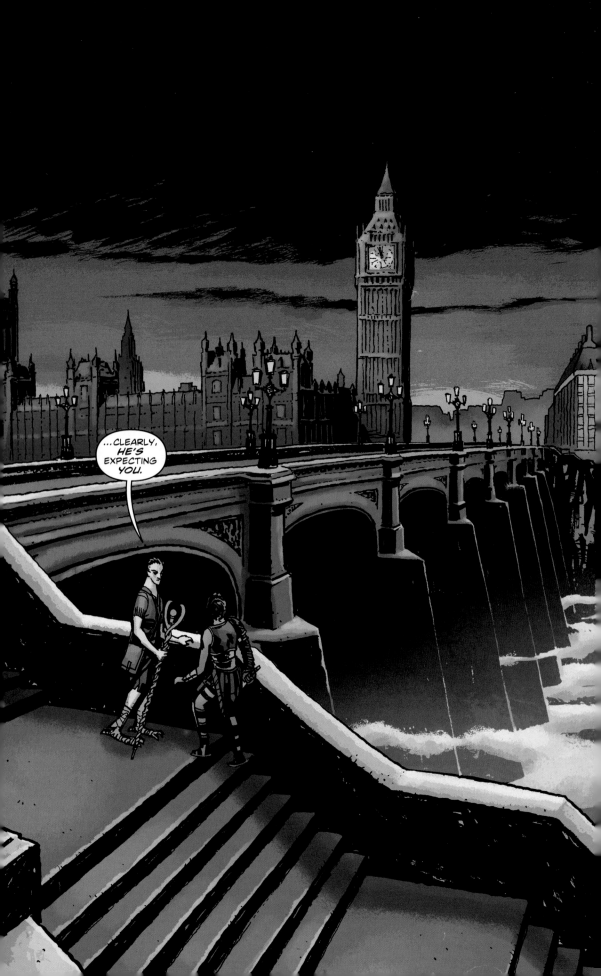

I CAN'T GET OVER THE EMPTINESS. I FIGURED, WELL...
THE DEAD WOULD BE *EVERYWHERE.*
THEY ARE.
WHERE ARE THEY?
EVERYWHERE.
THE WALLS, THE CLOUDS...
THE STREET UNDER YOUR FEET...
OH MY--
THE UNDERWORLD IS *MADE* OF SOULS.
--KRKKK.

HADES USES THE DEAD TO CONSTRUCT HIS KINGDOM?!
USES? HMMM... YOU'RE IMPLYING AN UNWILLINGNESS--
--TO BE WALKED ON, HERMES? DAMN RIGHT I AM!
YOU'RE YOUNG. I THINK THE CONCEPT OF ETERNITY IS SOMETHING YOU DON'T GRASP YET.
DIANA...BEING IMMORTAL IS A BLESSING, AND A TRAP.
A TRAP THAT MORTALS DON'T SHARE.
IMAGINE DYING, AND GAINING THE ABILITY TO BE ANYTHING.
ANYTHING FOR JUST A PIECE OF TIME, KNOWING THAT YOUR TIME TO REINVENT IS YOUR FOREVER.
NOT EXISTING IN A WORLD, BUT BEING THE WORLD...
IT HARDLY SEEMS LIKE BEING USED.
CLOK

HRRRRRRR

YOU CAN'T TELL ME *ANYONE* CHOSE TO BE THAT.

...FREE WILL IS A FUNNY THING.

EEEEEYYYAAAA

EEEEEE

?

VYYAAA

CHOK

CHOK

SSHHK

GET TO THE TREES.

I'M *NOT* LEAVING YOU--

I DON'T *NEED* YOUR PROTECTION, AND *I'M* NOT WHY WE'RE HERE!

NOW...

...FIND ZOLA!

KKRAK

KKRAK

I KNEW YOU WOULD COME.

HADES?
YOU STOLE SOMEONE I LOVE.
YOU LEFT ME NO CHOICE.
OH, I LEFT YOU?
I DON'T THINK SO.
THAT'S WHY YOU'RE HERE.
YOU MADE A BARGAIN.
HONOR IT, OR THE GIRL, ZOLA, WILL NEVER LEAVE.
NOR HER CHILD.
TRUTH BE TOLD, I DON'T UNDERSTAND WHY EITHER LIFE IS SO IMPORTANT TO YOU.
BECAUSE LIFE IS IMPORTANT.
NO, LIFE IS BRIEF.
TRULY, THAT'S ALL LIFE IS.

CHOK
CHOK
CHOK
CHOK
AND IN ITS BREVITY IS WHERE LIFE'S IMPORTANCE LIES.

EEEEYYYAA!
KRUNCH
I'D SAY THANKS, BUT...
IT LOOKS LIKE YOU ENJOYED THAT.
SO LET ME THANK *YOU*. AFTER BEING LAME, IT FELT GOOD TO BE GIVEN AN OPPORTUNITY.
THERE MAY BE ANOTHER ONE, JUST BEYOND THOSE TREES.
THE FIRST LIGHT WE'VE SEEN. LET'S--
--BE LIKE MOTHS?
NO, DIANA...
LET'S BE WHAT WE *ARE*.

THERE'S A STRANGELY VAGUE *FAMILIARITY* TO THIS...
OF COURSE. THE UNDERWORLD IS SHADOW. A DARK, FLUID REFLECTION OF WHAT'S REAL. NOT QUITE MEMORY...
MORE LIKE SOMETHING TRYING TO BE REMEMBERED.
YEAH... THAT'S WHAT IT IS. IT'S...
...ZOLA'S FARM.

WHO'S THERE? COME OUT WHERE I CAN SEE YOU, OR I SWEAR I'M GONNA JUST START FIRIN', SAME AS ALWAYS...
SAME AS ALWAYS?
ZOLA! IT'S--
...ZOLA?
HERMES?

WONDER WOMAN!

CALL ME DIANA... PLEASE, HOW MANY TIMES--

--NEVER! I *NEVER* GAVE UP HOPE! NOT AFTER THE FIRST *WEEK*, OR ALL THE *MONTHS*, NEVER...

I KNEW YOU'D COME FOR ME.

I *KNEW* IT. BUT...

WHAT *TOOK* YOU SO LONG!?

ZOLA... IT'S BEEN--

--*TOO* LONG. WE HAVE TO GET YOU OUT OF THIS PLACE.

WE, MESSENGER?

INTERESTING.
WHICH "WE" DO YOU SPEAK OF?
HADES...
IT'S A FAIR QUESTION.
YOU CAME HERE WITH *ONE,* BUT TO GET *ANOTHER.* SO...
WHICH CHILD OF ZEUS IS YOUR "WE"?
RHAAA!
--HERMES.

YOU WANT TO BE THE WE, WONDER WOMAN? FINE. FOR WE HAD A DEAL...
ME, WITH A QUEEN. TO PREVENT MY BROTHER AND ME FROM WARRING. SO HAVE YOU PERSUADED HERA TO MARRY US?
I DON'T THINK THAT'S GOING TO HAPPEN...
THEN ZOLA STAYS. AND HER CHILD WILL BE BORN IN SHADOWS...
I DESIRE TO SEE HOW THAT PLAYS OUT.
IT'S NOT ALL YOU DESIRE, THOUGH, IS IT, HADES?
YOU WANT A QUEEN.
I WAS PROMISED ONE.
BUT PERHAPS THERE'S SOMETHING ELSE YOU CAN GIVE ME.
SUCH AS?
THOSE PISTOLS... THEY BELONG TO EROS?
YES.

YES.
I WILL TAKE THEM IN TRADE. ZOLA AND HER CHILD WILL BE FREE TO GO.
WHAT ABOUT MY PROMISE OF HERA AS YOUR QUEEN?
YOU MEAN YOUR LIE? GIVE ME THE GUNS, AND IT'S FORGIVEN.
I HAVE YOUR WORD?
OF COURSE. I'LL HAVE WHAT I WANT.
LET'S GO, ZOLA.
WONDER WOMAN?

BLAM

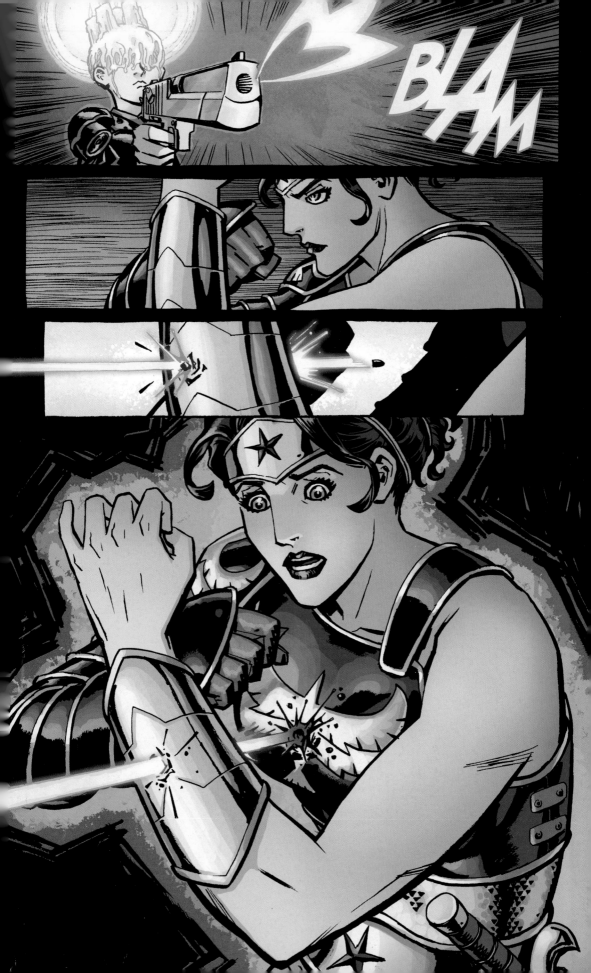

MESSENGER... INFORM OUR FAMILY, THERE WILL BE A WEDDING...
ZOLA...
I'M NOT LEAVING!
...YES... YOU ARE.
HERMES... GO...
"YES, HERMES... SHOO."
CAN'T YOU SEE SHE'S IN LOVE?

CLIFF-
CHIANG
2012

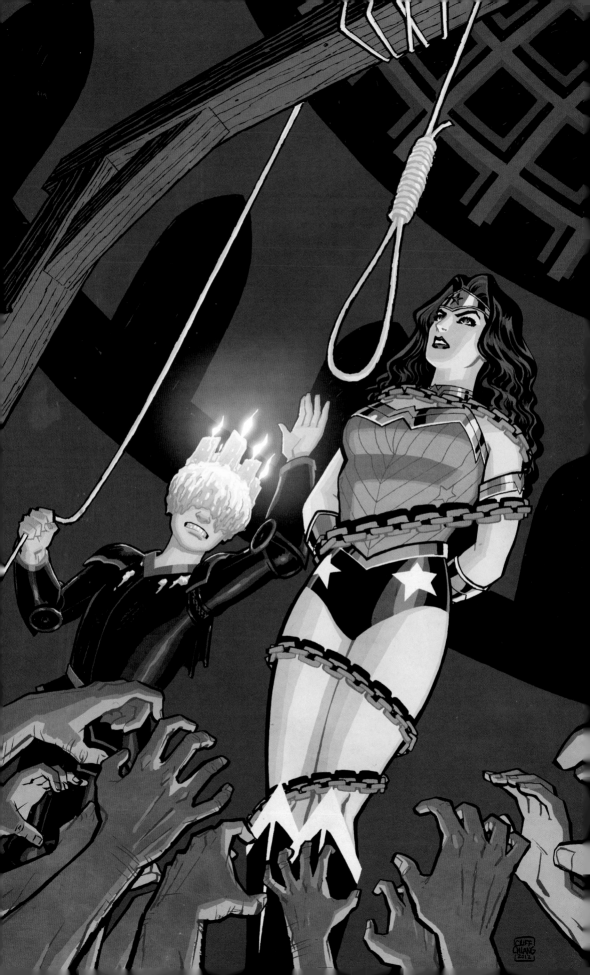

BROTHER...

≥OOF≥ HOW I LOATHE TO HEAR THAT WORD...

PLEASE, *WAR.* WHY MUST YOU BE SO...

COMBATIVE?

HA. MY DEAR STRIFE... PERHAPS IT'S BECAUSE YOU BRING OUT THE *WORST*--AND THE *BEST* IN ME.

THANK YOU. NOW, ABOUT THESE IMPENDING NUPTIALS...I'M LOOKING FOR AN ESCORT.

WELL, IT WON'T BE ME. A POLICY--ONE WEDDING PER CUSTOMER. IF THE FIRST DOESN'T WORK OUT...

THEN I WON'T BE BOTHERED WATCHING THE BEGINNING OF THE *NEXT* FAILURE.

BUT WAR... YOU AND I TOGETHER, WE *MAKE* THE PARTY. YOU SHOULD RECONSIDER, BECAUSE I'M SURE...

...IT'LL BE A BLAST.

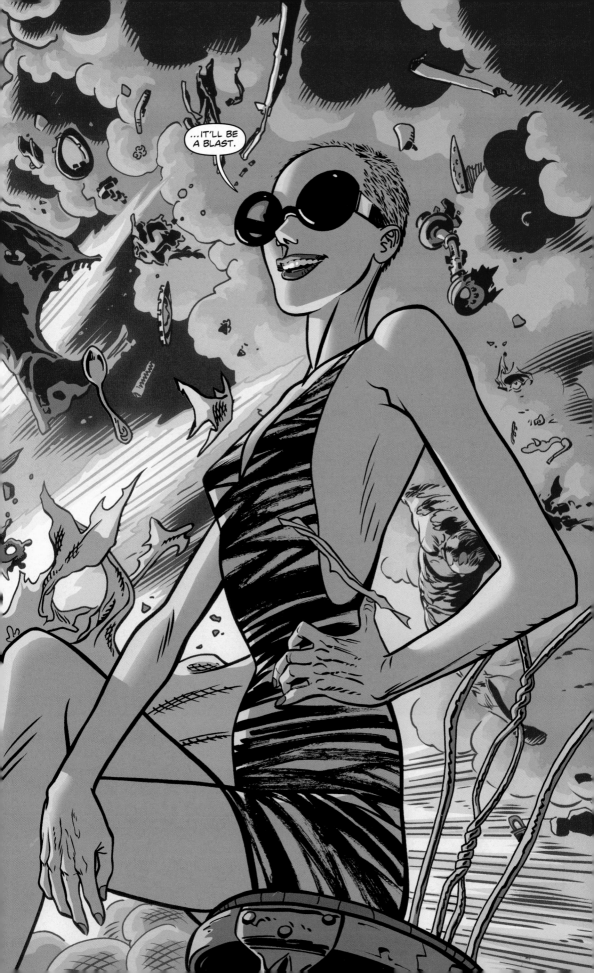

HELL CAN MARRY WHOMEVER. I DON'T CARE.

EVEN IF YOUR *WHOM* IS WONDER WOMAN?

GRRRR

...YES, EVEN IF.

NOW IF YOU'LL EXCUSE ME...

I HAVE TO TEND TO OTHER THINGS I DON'T CARE ABOUT.

MOUNT ETNA.

BOLLOCKS!

THERE WAS NO CHOICE. *DIANA* UNDERSTOOD. GIVEN THE CIRCUMSTANCES--

--DON' YEA *DARE* SAY I WOULDA DONE THE SAME, MESSENGER.

LENNOX, WONDER WOMAN'S GOAL WAS TO RESCUE THIS MORTAL GIRL.

MY *NAME'S* ZOLA.

AND YOU'VE BEEN RESCUED. DIDN'T ANY OF YOU STOP TO THINK THERE WOULD BE A COST?

US?! WHAT ABOUT *YOU?*

YOU GAVE MY *GUNS* TO WONDER WOMAN, AND THEY WERE USED *AGAINST* HER! WHAT WERE YOU *THINKING?*

HMM. WHAT *WAS* I...?

HOLY... CAN YOU IDIOTS STOP ARGUING AND START FIGURING OUT HOW WE'RE GONNA *SAVE* DIANA?!

WE'RE NOT, ZOLA.

I SWORE I WOULD PROTECT YOU, AND GOING *BACK*--

WOULD BE BREAKING AN OATH?

KEEP YER OATH, I'LL BREAK YER NECK.
TRY, AND YOU'LL QUICKLY FIND YOUR WAY TO THE UNDERWORLD WITHOUT THE NEED OF AN ESCORT.
WELL THEN, WE'RE ALL VERY LUCKY NOT TO NEED ONE.
AND YOU, GIRL, ARE VERY LUCKY TO HAVE A CHAMPION SO STEADFAST, EVEN THOUGH IT PAINS HIM TO BE.
DON'T WORRY ABOUT WONDER WOMAN. SHE DOESN'T NEED SAVING.
HOW WE GONNA GO TO HELL WITHOUT THE MESSENGER TAKING US?
I'VE BEEN INVITED. YOU'LL BE MY GUEST.
HERMES...
HEAT OF THE MOMENT.
YEA.
THEN IT'S SETTLED, AND I HAVE WORK TO DO.
I MEAN, IT WOULD BE RUDE OF US TO SHOW UP...

"...WITHOUT A GIFT."

DOES IT HURT?

NO...

IT'S A *HOLE*...

IT ACHES.

WELL... I'M SURE MY LORD WILL HAPPILY *FILL IT* IN YOUR WEDDING CHAMBER.

YES...THOUGH I DON'T KNOW *WHAT* MAKES HIM HAPPY.

HADES? GIVEN ETERNITY, YOU MIGHT HAVE A CHANCE OF FINDING OUT.

HAVE YOU BEEN WITH HIM A WHILE?

I'VE...

ETERNITY DOESN'T END, MY LADY.

HE'S DONE SOMETHING FOR YOU.

HE HAS?

COME SEE.

OH...

PARADISE ISLAND...

PLEASE LET MY LORD KNOW THAT I'D...

HIS LOVE CAN BE CLUMSY. AND THOUGH HE MEANS WELL...

IT CAN ALSO BE *CRUEL.*

DON'T WORRY. I'LL INFORM HIM THAT YOU'D RATHER NOT BE REMINDED OF HOME. THAT...

DRIP

GIRL... YOU'RE BLEEDING...

I'M SORRY, MY LADY.

SORRY? WHO DID THIS TO YOU?

HE... WOULDN'T LET ME LEAVE.

IN TRYING TO ESCAPE, I DAMNED MYSELF, AND HE WILL *NEVER* LET ME FORGET...

WHO? TELL ME!

I DID! I *DID* THIS TO MYSELF!

MY NAME IS PERSEPHONE!

I WAS HADES' WIFE ONCE!

"I AM *SO* FREAKED OUT BY ALL OF THIS..."

THAT'S UNDERSTANDABLE, ZOLA. WHILE MONTHS PASSED FOR YOU IN HELL, HERE IT WAS ONLY A FEW DAYS.

BOTH REALITIES ARE REAL, THOUGH IT MAY BE HARD FOR YOU TO GRASP.

UM, HELLO? IN CASE YOU HAVEN'T NOTICED, HERMES, I DO PRETTY WELL WITH ALL THE CRAZY GODS AND WEIRD MYTHOLOGY CRAP.

BUT--

WONDER WOMAN SAVED YOUR LIFE-- MINE, TOO. AND IT KINDA SUCKS YOU WON'T RETURN THE FAVOR.

I'M HAVING A HARD TIME DEALING WITH *THAT.*

THEN YOU SHOULDN'T-- ESPECIALLY BECAUSE IT'S NOT YOUR BURDEN TO CARRY.

?

APHRODITE!

WHOA.

A PLEASURE AS ALWAYS?
INDEED IT IS.
ZOLA, THIS IS HEPHAESTUS' WIFE.
YER KIDDING ME...
THE SMITH HAS HIS CHARMS, GIRL...
APHRODITE, THIS IS MY CHARGE, ZOLA. SHE'S--
BLOSSOMING. FROM ZEUS' SEED.
I'VE...I'VE NEVER FELT MORE UGLY IN MY LIFE...
UGLY? BUT YOU'RE BEAUTIFUL! NEVER FORGET THAT!
EASY FOR YOU TO SAY.
TRUE, THAT.
ZOLA, I OVERHEARD WHAT YOU WERE SAYING...AND, IF I CAN GIVE SOME ADVICE...
IT'S WRONG TO FAULT THE MESSENGER, WITHOUT CONSIDERING THE MESSAGE.
ARE YOU GOING TO HELL WITH THE REST OF THEM?
ME? NO. THERE ISN'T SPACE IN HELL FOR LOVE. IT'S TOO CLUTTERED...

"...WITH MEMORIES AND REGRETS."
JUST A FEW ARE COMING.
I'M DISAPPOINTED.
THAT'S... YOUR... NATURE.
ARE YOU SAYING ALL OF MY FAMILY COULD ATTEND THIS WEDDING, AND I'D STILL FIND SOMETHING LACKING?
I'M... SO...
YOU... WOULD.
HUNGRY...
PERHAPS YOU'RE RIGHT, FATHER. ONE OF THEM WOULD SAY SOMETHING DREADFUL, PUT ME OFF--
AM I EARLY?

STRIFE.
YES, YOU'RE EARLY, BUT--
I WOULDN'T BE ME UNLESS I WAS!
OR LATE. BUT NEVER ON TIME.
UNCLE. KISSES.
I'M SO HAPPY YOU'VE FOUND LOVE, AND THERE'S GOING TO BE A WEDDING...
SHOT GUN AS IT IS.
YOU'RE HAPPY? THAT GIVES ME PAUSE...
WELL THEN, THAT GIVES YOU SOMETHING IN COMMON WITH YOUR BRIDE, THOUGH HERS...
ARE CLAWED.
CAN YOU OFFER ME A DRINK?

THERE'S *WINE*...

YOU CERTAINLY HAVE A UNIQUE SENSE OF *STYLE,* UNCLE.

CHEERS.

WELL, THAT MAY HAVE TO DO WITH YOUR *TASTE* IN WOMEN. I MEAN, YOU SEEM TO BE DRAWN TO THE HARD-TO-GET.

WHAT I'M DRAWN TO, I *DO* GET.

NOW, THOUGH IT'S NOT MY PLACE, LET ME APOLOGIZE FOR MOTHER AND WAR NOT ATTENDING.

THEY AREN'T THE *ONLY* ONES FROM OUR FAMILY WHO WON'T BE COMING.

BUT IS IT WHAT YOU DESERVE?

I'D JUST *HATE* FOR YOU TO BE DISAPPOINTED BY LOVE...

AGAIN.

SAY... MAYBE THERE'S A *WAY*...

SO WHAT'S OUR PLAN OF ATTACK, HEPHAESTUS?
WE FIND OUR SEATS.
WE DON' FIND DIANA?
WHY? WE KNOW WHERE SHE'LL BE.
BUT AIN'T THE POINT NOT TO LET HER GET THERE?
WE'LL SEE.
'OW? THE LIGHT-- IT'S BLINDING. WHERE IS IT COMING FROM?
IN LIGHT OF HIS FAMILY'S REFUSAL, HADES MUST HAVE INVITED...

...EVERY SOUL HE HAS.

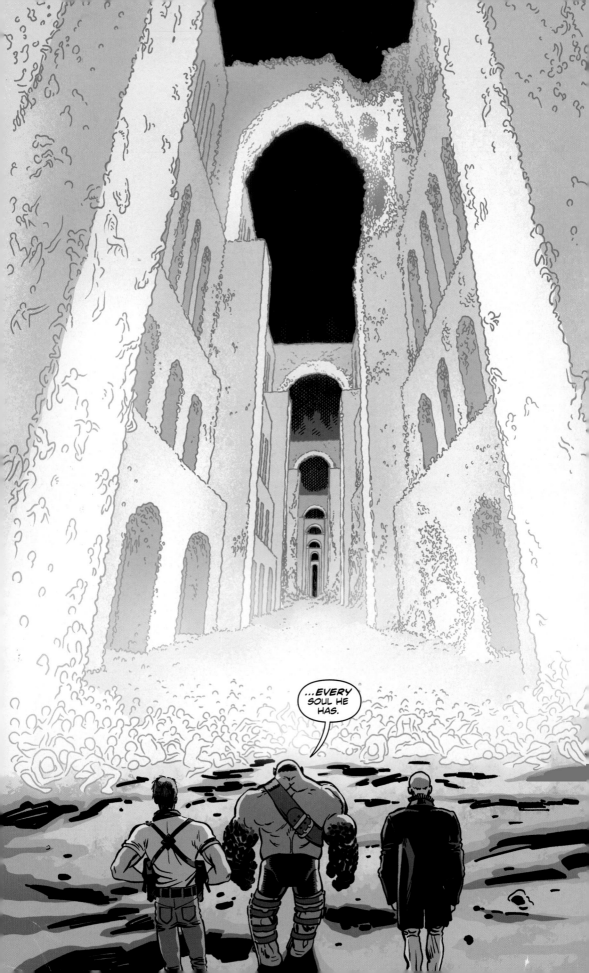

BE STILL, WE'RE ALMOST DONE.
THERE.
FINISHED?
NOT YET...
IF YOU DARE SHAME YOUR HUSBAND...
WE WILL RIP YOU TO SHREDS AND FEED THEM FOR ETERNITY TO EVERY RAT THAT HAS EVER EXISTED AND HAS YET TO BE BORN.
FATHER...
YOUR BRIDE.
MY BRIDE. MY, MY, DON'T YOU LOOK...
WONDERFUL.

THIS IS SO BEAUTIFUL. IT'S ALL I COULD WANT IN A WEDDING, MY LORD.

THAT'S VERY KIND OF YOU TO SAY.

MY WORDS WEREN'T MEANT TO JUST BE KIND.

WELL, FEW ARE.

I'D LIKE TO BE HONEST WITH YOU.

PLEASE.

I'M INCAPABLE OF LOVE.

I DON'T BELIEVE THAT.

I...AM NOT ENTIRELY SURE. I CHOSE TO LIVE HERE BECAUSE I WANTED TO BE ALONE.

BUT YOU DON'T.

AND I'M *NOT*. OF ALL THE REALMS, THE HEAVENS AND EARTH...

IT'S BEEN BROUGHT TO MY ATTENTION THAT YOU MAY NOT *ACTUALLY* LOVE ME.

THAT THIS COULD BE AN ELABORATE RUSE ON YOUR PART, USED TO SECURE THE FREEDOM OF THE MORTAL GIRL.

IS YOUR WILL THAT STRONG?

THAT WOULD BE VERY FOOLISH OF ME, LORD HADES.

INDEED. YOU REALIZE THAT I WOULD FIND ZOLA AGAIN, AND DRAG HER AND THE CHILD BACK...

OR WORSE?

I DO.

NOT *YET*, MY DEAR...

WE HAVEN'T REACHED THE ALTAR.

MY HEART BELONGS TO YOU, MY LORD.

WELL, SEEING THAT'S SOMETHING I WOUNDED...

I'M IN NEED OF YOUR TRUTH.

I JUST TOLD--

YES, YOU DID. BUT A TONGUE CAN BE MANY THINGS. MOST OF ALL, CUNNING.

SO I THOUGHT, PERHAPS WE WOULD BREAK FROM TRADITION.

THAT YOU WOULD WEAR YOUR RING *BEFORE* THE CEREMONY.

IF THAT WILL PROVE MY LOVE, THEN I ACCEPT.

GOOD.

BEHOLD, YOUR *WEDDING RING.*
AROUND YOUR NECK, YOU WILL PROFESS YOUR LOVE.
OR NOT.

YOUR TRUTH, THEN, WILL BIND ME...

OR *HANG* YOU.

"YOU'VE PROMISED YOUR LOVE..."
BUT I NEED MORE.
BUT HADES... WHAT CAN MEAN MORE THAN A PROMISE?
PROOF. YOUR LASSO--
LEGEND HAS IT THAT ANYONE BOUND BY IT IS BOUND BY THE TRUTH.
SO... YOU DON'T TRUST ME?
THAT SOUNDS AWFUL.
SO LET'S SAY... GIVEN YOUR ANSWER, I WON'T HAVE TO.

DO YOU LOVE ME, WONDER WOMAN?
HELL...
I DO LOVE YOU.

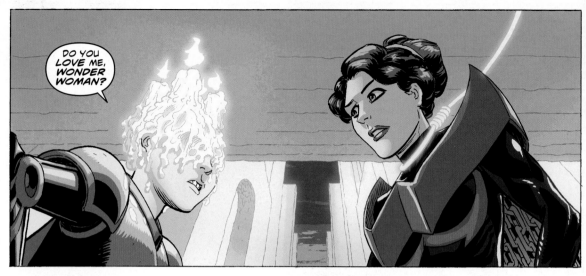

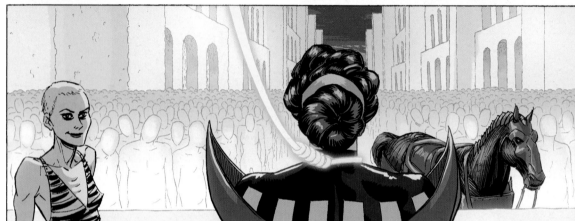

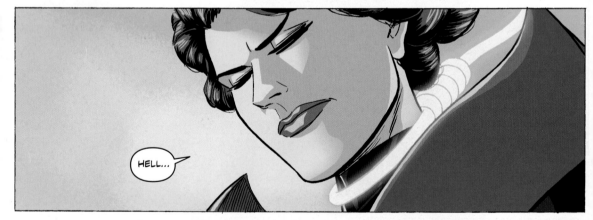

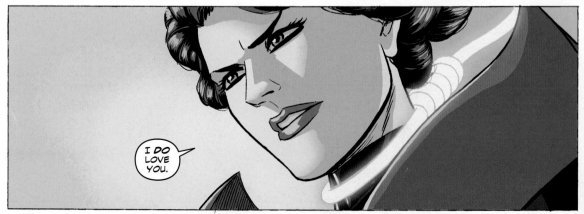

THEN IT'S SETTLED.

DIANA OF THEMYSCIRA, PRINCESS OF THE AMAZONS, I NOW BIND YOU--

BIND ME?

SNAP

THWIPP

WITH PROOF--NOT *TRUST*?

I WON'T BE BOUND THAT WAY TO ANY MAN...

WOMAN...

OR GOD.

DO YOU KNOW WHERE YOU ARE?
YOU CAN'T ESCAPE ME.
I DON'T CARE WHAT YOU ARE--
I KNOW WHO I AM...
AND I CAN'T ESCAPE THAT.

I WILL *FIND* YOUR GIRL ZOLA, AND I WILL--
--FIND THOSE I TRUST TO PROTECT HER *WITH* HER.
AND THEY WILL NOT GO DOWN WITHOUT A *FIGHT*.
I WILL KILL YOU.
KILL ME, LOVE ME, WHAT'S THE DIFFERENCE?
YOU WILL TRY.
AND YOU PROBABLY WILL SUCCEED.
BUT IT *WON'T* BE EASY.
TRUST ME.

RRRAAAAHHH

WE **WARNED** YOU!

THERE'S NO LEAVING FATHER'S REALM WITHOUT HIS RELEASE! YOU'RE TRAPPED HERE FOR **ETERNITY!**

YOUR LIFE IS **OVER!**

YOU'RE NOTHING BUT **MEAT** NOW.

MEAT?

MEET AN **AMAZON.**

EH. I'D SAY THE WEDDING IS OFF.

JUST AS GOOD.

WHUMP

YEEAAAH

CRACK

WHAM

RIGHT, THAT.

WHAT ARE YOU *DOING* HERE--? YOU SHOULD BE WITH ZOLA!

HERMES IS.

OH. YEAH.

SORRY, I ASSUMED IT WAS ALL OF YOU.

STILL, THIS IS *MY* FIGHT. YOU SHOULDN'T HAVE COME--

I THINK YER RIGHT...

I HOPE I'M WRONG.

AH... I SEE NOW.

YOU JUST WANTED TO WELCOME OUR GUESTS.

I'M SORRY, HEPHAESTUS, BUT THERE'S BEEN A CHANGE OF PLANS. THERE WILL BE NO WEDDING. IN ITS STEAD...

AN EXECUTION.

YOU CONDEMN ME, LORD?--FOR TELLING THE TRUTH?

YES, MY BRIDE...

I DO.

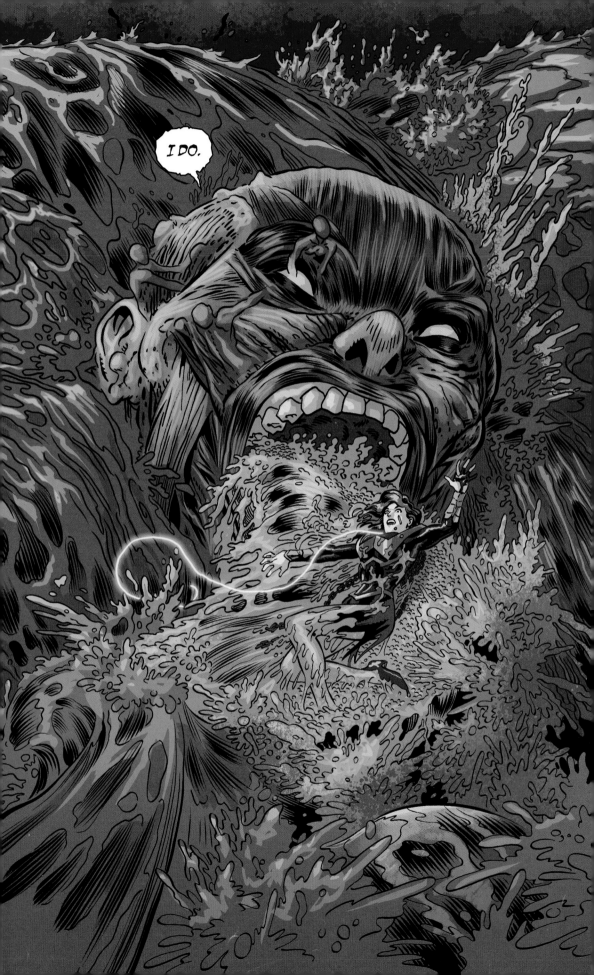

YOU WILL *NEVER* LEAVE HELL, WONDER WOMAN.

YOU WILL LIVE FOR ETERNITY...

BEING CONSUMED BY ME.

OVER AND OVER AND--

YOU *TOO*, STRIFE?

WHY CAN'T ANY OF YOU LET ME FIGHT THIS *ALONE?!*

YOU'RE *KIDDING*, RIGHT?

I MEAN, BEING *CONSUMED*, THAT DOES HAVE A CERTAIN *ROMANTICISM* TO IT, BUT *OVER* AND *OVER* AGAIN...

THE *BETWEEN* BITS. THAT'S *MESSY*, EVEN FOR *YOU*.

CAN'T IT JUST BE *MY* MESS?!

EWW...

LET HER *FIGHT*.

SHE CAN'T WIN.
WINNING IS NOT ALWAYS MY GOAL.
THEN WHY FIGHT?
BECAUSE *THIS* BATTLE...
I WILL *NEVER* LOSE.
YOU LIED TO ME.
NO, I DIDN'T. I DO LOVE YOU.
HELL...
I *LOVE*.
EVERYONE.

THAT'S RIDICULOUS--

MAYBE. CERTAINLY TO SOMEONE INCAPABLE OF IT.

SMITH...STRIFE BEING HERE, OF COURSE. A WEDDING IS SOMETHING SHE WOULDN'T MISS.

BUT YOU... I THOUGHT YOU AGREED TO COME TO THIS WEDDING-- WHEN THE REST OF OUR FAMILY DECLINED-- BECAUSE YOU DESPISE THEM EVEN MORE THAN I.

I...

DESPISE IS A STRONG WORD.

WE... DISAPPOINT ME.

HOW SO?

BECAUSE WE ARE CAPABLE OF SO MUCH BETTER.

WE FIGHT, AND IT'S NOT BECAUSE WE LOVE EACH OTHER.

BUT IT SHOULD BE.

YOU'RE A SENTIMENTAL FOOL. IS THAT WHY MY SISTER THREW YOU TO THE ROCKS?

NO, UNCLE...

IT'S BECAUSE MY MOTHER COULDN'T LOVE ME.

AND WONDER WOMAN CAN'T LOVE *ME!* EVEN USING EROS' PISTOLS...

HADES... I BELIEVE-- I'M NOT SURE-- BUT...

YOU COULD FIRE THEM AT ANYONE, AND THE RESULTS WOULD BE THE SAME.

YOU CAN'T MAKE ANYONE LOVE YOU UNLESS YOU LOVE YOURSELF.

IT'S TRUE. NO ONE LOVES HIMSELF MORE THAN EROS.

FATHER?

AND I LOVE YOU EVEN MORE THAN THAT, MY SON.

SO YOU LOVE ME, BUT YOU WON'T BE MY BRIDE?
THAT'S TRUE.
BUT YOU LOVE ME?
...
I DO.
NO. DON'T TOUCH ME...
JUST GO.

SO THERE WON'T BE A WEDDING? *THAT* MEANS NO *DIVOR--*

GO.

THUMP

THUMP

HELL...

I MADE THIS FOR YOU. DON'T LET IT GO TO WASTE.

WHY DO I GET THE FEELING YOU HAD THIS ALL PLANNED?

I WOULDN'T KNOW.

BUT YOU DID?

PLANS... WHEN DO THEY EVER WORK OUT?

EROS-- IF I MAY?

≥HMMMPH≤

HOW'S YOUR AIM?

MY AIM...?

BLAM

"IT'S TRUE."

KRAKOOM
OLYMPUS.
MOTHER, I'M BACK-- AND LET ME SAY, YOU MISSED ONE HELL OF A FABULOUS TIME...
DID I? OH WELL. I'M SURE THERE'LL BE OTHERS.
WHAT WONDER WOMAN DID TO THAT LITTLE IMP WAS PRICELESS!
PLEASE, STRIFE, THERE'S ALWAYS A PRICE FOR EVERYTHING WE DO.
AND YOU WON'T GET MY GOAT, SINGING THE AMAZON'S PRAISES.
OH, BUT IT'S SUCH A SONG... I DARE SAY, I'M BEGINNING TO LIKE MY BABY SISTER.
I WOULDN'T GET TOO ATTACHED...
FOR THERE'S NOW A PRICE ON THAT BABY SHE'S SWORN TO PROTECT.

YOU DIDN'T!
IF THE AMAZON MEANS TO STAY HER COURSE, I DOUBT SHE'LL SURVIVE.
CARE TO WAGER?
I STRUCK A BARGAIN TONIGHT, DAUGHTER...
FOR SOMETHING THAT MEANS MUCH, MUCH MORE THAN THE LIFE OF ONE--OR TWO--OF YOUR FATHER'S BASTARD OFFSPRING.
BUT I STRUCK IT ANYWAY...
WITH ONE OF THEM.
"SO I WOULDN'T BET AGAINST ME."
KRAKOOM

COLOMA, MICHIGAN.
THE TREES ARE HEAVY, SISTER.
I REALIZE THIS IS A BUSY TIME FOR YOU...
BUT WE NEED TO TALK.
ABOUT?
A CHANGE OF THE GUARD WE MUST DISCUSS, DEMETER.
THEN LET'S, PLEASE.
WHAT'S ON YOUR MIND...

...ARTEMIS?

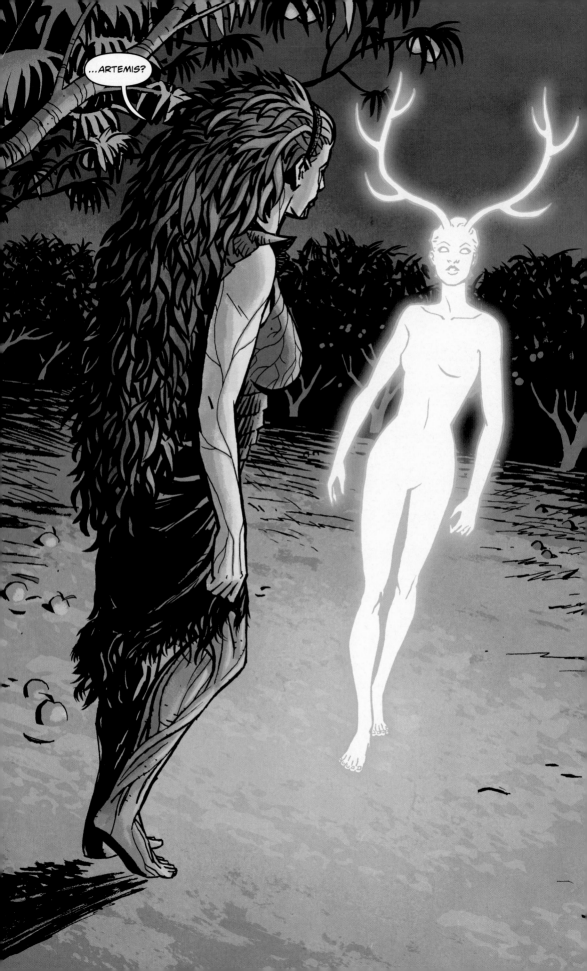

HARVEST... ZEUS' EMPTY SEAT, IT'S GOING TO BE *FILLED.*

IT NEEDS TO BE. THE HEAVENS WITH-OUT A RULER CAN ONLY BRING CHAOS.

AGAIN.

AND WE DON'T WANT *THAT.*

NO, WE DON'T.

WHAT *IS* IT WE WANT INSTEAD?

MY BROTHER HAS INFORMED ME OF A DISTURBING *PROPHECY...* ONE THAT HAS US BEATEN BY OUR OWN BLOOD.

THAT'S NOT A *PROPHECY...*

...THAT'S AN INEVITABILITY.

THERE'S NO ROOM FOR IMPROVISATION IN YOU, IS THERE?

MOON, THERE'S BIRTH AND THERE'S DEATH, AND IN BETWEEN...

"...IT'S ALL IMPROVISATION."
OLIVEBURN, VIRGINIA.
LOOK, HERMES, I'LL BE FINE.
HERE?
REALLY?
57
DING
REALLY. YOU WANTED ME TO SEE A DOCTOR?...
SO, I'M SEEING ONE.
WHAT DO YOU THINK YOU'RE DOING?
NOT LETTING YOU OUT OF MY SIGHT.
OH YES--
YOU ARE.
HERMES...

I DON'T FEEL GOOD ABOUT THIS, DIANA.

GIVEN THE STAGE OF HER PREGNANCY, WE *ALL* INSISTED THAT ZOLA SEE A DOCTOR.

TOO BAD WE DIDN' FIGURE SHE'D INSIST ON SEEIN' 'ER *OWN*.

SHE'S JUST TRYING TO EXERT A LITTLE CONTROL ON A LIFE THAT'S SPUN OUT OF IT, LENNOX.

THE LEAST WE CAN DO IS SUPPORT HER.

BUT YOU 'AVE *FRIENDS*, ACCESS TO BETTER MEDICAL--

I *DO* HAVE FRIENDS, TRUE...

AND ONE OF THEM IS SEEING THE DOCTOR *SHE'S* CHOSEN TO RIGHT NOW.

ZOLA IS CARRYING ZEUS' BABY...

HAH! WHAT IF IN THE ULTRASOUND, IT'S DISCOVERED THE LITTLE NIPPPER'S GOT A TAIL? OR *WINGS*?

I'M JUST *SAYIN'*...

AND I *DON'T* FEEL GOOD ABOUT IT.

?

WHA'SSIS-- AN ECLIPSE?

THERE WASN'T A FORECAST OF--

NO...
DIANA, LOOK...
THE MOON ISN'T PASSING OVER THE SUN...
VROOOOM VROOOOM
THEY'VE JOINED.
AND I FEEL VERY VERY BAD ABOUT--
IF YOU FEEL VERY VERY BAD NOW, MESSENGER, JUST IMAGINE WHAT IT'LL BE LIKE IF YOU DON'T GIVE US WHAT WE WANT.
OR, IMAGINE FEELING NOTHING.
THAT IS WHAT IT'S LIKE TO BE DEAD, NO?

APOLLO.

ARTEMIS.

HERMES.

WONDER WOMAN.

AND...

I APOLOGIZE, I DON'T KNOW YOUR NAME.

IT'S LENNOX.

I'LL NOTE IT ON YOUR TOMBSTONE.

SUN AND MOON...

I'M SURPRISED YOU WOULD TAKE AN INTEREST IN ONE OF ZEUS' DALLIANCES...

SEEING YOU'RE BORN FROM THE SAME.

MESSENGER, I HAVE NO INTEREST IN THE GIRL, OR THE CHILD SHE CARRIES.

BUT THEY ARE A MEANS TO AN END.

PITY IF YOU MEAN THEM TO BE YOURS.

AMAZON... YOU'VE BEEN THROUGH MUCH, AND YOUR BEHAVIOR HAS BEEN STUNNING, ACTUALLY.

YOU'VE MADE FOOLS OF MY UNCLES. AND OUR QUEEN.

THAT'S NOT POSSIBLE ANY LONGER. YOU'VE HAD YOUR FUN.

IT'S TIME FOR YOU TO STEP DOWN.

REALLY?

I'VE NEVER FELT MORE LIKE STEPPING UP.

STEP, THEN...

INTO YOUR GRAVE.

LENNOX!

I'M ALL RIGHT, LUV.

NOTHING A VISIT TO THE HABERDASHER WON'T FIX.

GAAH!

WHAM

I PROMISED TO *PROTECT* THAT GIRL, APOLLO...

AND I PROMISED TO *DELIVER* HER.

I WON'T BREAK MINE.

KRAK

KRUNK

THEN I'LL BREAK *YOU.*

WHUMP

WHAM

WHAT IS *YOUR* INTEREST IN THIS, MESSENGER?

CERTAINLY NOT THE MORTAL.

SO WHAT *IS* IT ABOUT HER CHILD?

IS IT THE ONE SPOKEN OF IN THE PROPHECY? THE CHILD OF ZEUS THAT WILL *MURDER* FOR A THRONE?

IF IT IS... HOW IS IT DIFFERENT FROM YOU OR YOUR BROTHER?

THUK

THUK

THUK

INTENTIONS, MESSENGER. IT'S ALWAYS IN--

WHAM

CRACK

BLOODY HELL...

MY MY, LENNOX, AREN'T YOU SOMETHING...

WHEN I MENTIONED YOUR TOMBSTONE, I DIDN'T REALIZE I COULD CARVE IT *OUT* OF YOU.

TELL ME-- SINCE YOU INSIST ON DYING-- HOW LONG HAVE YOU BEEN ALIVE?

TWENTY-THREE YEARS.

HMM. THEN I SUPPOSE I FORGIVE YOU YOUR ARROGANCE. SO SHALL WE CALL YOUR OPPOSITION TO ME...
A YOUTHFUL INDISCRETION, OR A TRAGIC LESSON?
...I WON'T LEAVE THE NAMING UP TO YOU.
YOU DON'T HAVE A CHOICE. I HAVE A DESTINY-- AND A PROPHECY-- TO FORESTALL.
THERE'S A STORM ON THE HORIZON. ONE THAT I PLAN TO...
VRM VRM
...FACE DOWN.
KNOW, WE ARE GODS... AND WE WON'T BE DESTROYED. NOT BY OURSELVES...
OR... BY ME?
CRASH

HA...HOW PERFECT.

BOOOm

NICE TO MEET *YOU*, TOO.

OH MY GOD--

--HERMES!

MOON, WE HAVE WHAT WE CAME FOR...

"LET'S RIDE."

DIANA...

I'LL LIVE...

BECAUSE HE LET ME...

DIDN'T JUST RUB OUR NOSES IN IT...

...BUT *BLOODIED* THEM AS WELL.

ARE YOU...?

DONE. BARELY HOLDING IT TOGETHER.

NO GOOD NOW. TO YOU...

...OR THE GIRL."
OLYMPUS.
WELCOME TO HEAVEN, ZOLA.
AM... AM I *DEAD?*
NOT YET.
NOR FOR A LONG, LONG TIME TO COME. BY THE TIME *I'M* FINISHED WITH YOU, DEATH WILL SEEM AS A PRECIOUS GIFT.
HE-- WHOEVER HE WAS--DIDN'T TELL ME HE WAS *MARRIED!*
WOULD THAT HAVE MADE A DIFFERENCE?
...
PROBABLY NOT.
HA! YOU *HAVE* TO ADMIRE HER AUDACITY, MOTHER.
I DON'T HAVE TO DO A *THING!*
YES, HERA, YOU *DO...*

AND MY FATHER'S SEED.
ME HIS THRONE, MY QUEEN.
YOUR QUEEN?
FATHER'S THRONE--IN EXCHANGE FOR HIS MISTRESS AND THEIR WHELP? MOTHER, FAR BE IT FROM ME TO INTERFERE WITH--
THEN BE FAR FROM ME, STRIFE.
I'M QUITE COMFORTABLE WITH THIS BARGAIN.
APOLLO. BASTARD SON...
THE THRONE IS YOURS.
I WON'T STAND IN YOUR WAY.
WELL, THEN...

...I WILL.

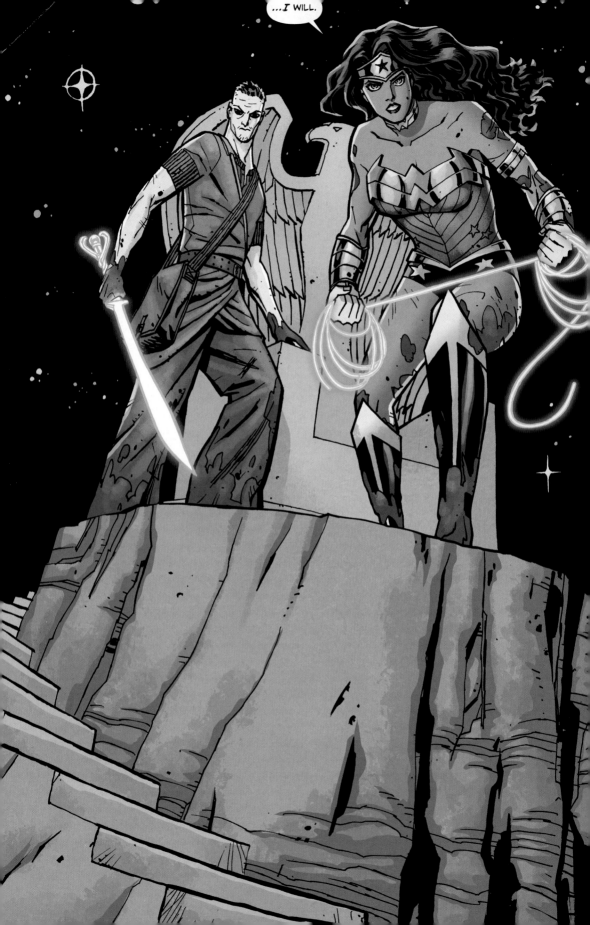

CLIFF
CHIANG
2012

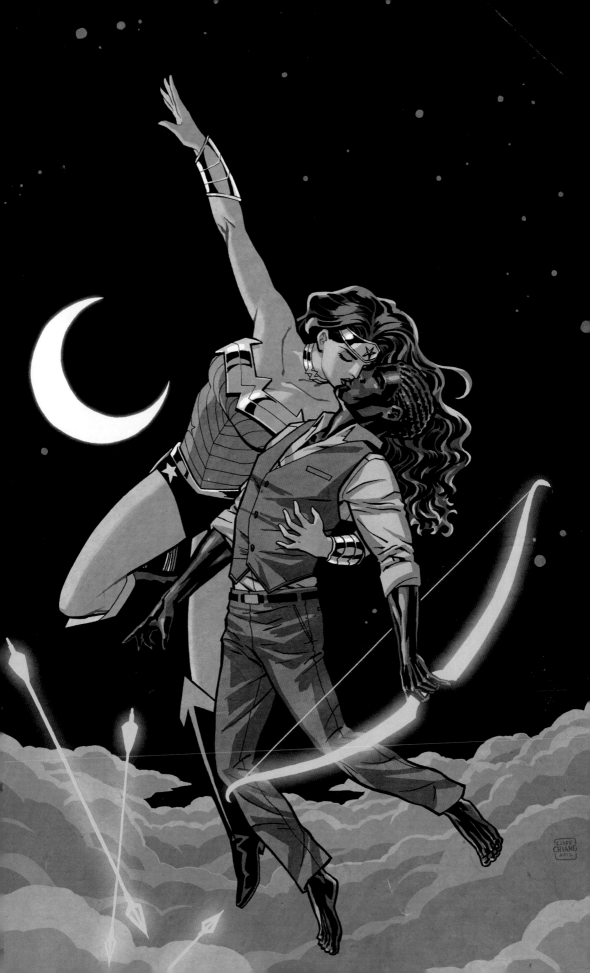

MY ORACLES HAVE TOLD ME OF A STORM BREWING OFF THE SHORES OF REALITY...
ONE THAT THREATENS TO DESTROY THIS FAMILY. IF WE ARE TO WITHSTAND IT, OLYMPUS WILL NEED A STRONG HAND.
THAT WOULD BE YOU, APOLLO?
PRECISELY.
THE THRONE IS MY DESTINY. MY BIRTHRIGHT.
B-SHU
AND I WON'T BE DENIED. THERE'S TOO MUCH AT STAKE.
INDEED, APOLLO. THE LIFE OF MY FRIEND.
AND HER UNBORN CHILD.

WONDER WOMAN OVER FAMILY, HERMES? YOU LEAVE ME WITH NO CHOICE BUT TO FORGO TRADITIONAL WISDOM...
AND KILL THE MESSENGER.
PLEASE BROTHER, ALLOW *ME*...
I WON'T BE SO GENTLE THIS TIME.
NOR I, ARTEMIS.
IS THAT A THREAT, AMAZON?

IT'S A PROMISE.

YOU'RE GOOD, AMAZON, BUT YOU CAN'T POSSIBLY BEST ME IN COMBAT.

YOUR ARROGANCE WILL DRIVE ME TO BE *BETTER*.

BUT NOT GOOD ENOUGH.

HOW CAN YOU BE SO CERTAIN?

BECAUSE IN YOUR *HEART*...

...YOU'RE *TOO* GOOD.

"COME, MY DEAR ZOLA..."

...IT'S TIME TO MEET YOUR FATE.
OH...
OHHH!
MOTHER, WITH THE THRONE OF HEAVEN AT STAKE, YOU'RE MORE CONCERNED WITH MAKING A MORTAL WET HERSELF?...
I SUPPOSE IT'S NOT UNLIKE YOU...
HER WATER HAS BROKEN. AND THE THRONE OF HEAVEN IS JUST FINE.
APOLLO'S AMBITION HAS BLINDED HIM TO A FACT I KNOW ABOUT MY HUSBAND...
ZEUS BELIEVES HE'S ENTITLED TO EVERYTHING. HE'S A MAN-- HE CAN'T NOT EXIST. AND BEING ONE, HE CAN'T LET ANYONE TAKE WHAT IS HIS.
WHEN APOLLO SITS? ZEUS WILL RETURN TO WIPE THAT STAIN OFF HIS SEAT.
I DARE SAY YOU HAVE EVEN MORE TRUST IN FATHER THAN HE DOES HIMSELF...
WE ARE GODS.
I'M NOT A FOOL, STRIFE. I DON'T TRUST HIM...

BUT I HAVE FAITH IN THE ONLY MAN I LOVE.
YOU, GIRL...
DID YOU LOVE HIM?
UHHH...
FOR ABOUT AN HOUR, I GUESS.
THAT DOESN'T SEEM NEARLY LONG ENOUGH...
NO, IT DOESN'T. SO DO TRY TO LOVE HIM, AS YOU GROW OLD.
OLD, AS WILL THE SCREAMING BEAST OF YOUR UNION, UMBILICALLY TAILING YOU FOR ALL TIME, BOUNCING OFF THE CLIFFS...
...AS YOU FALL FOR ALL ETERNITY.

ZOLA!
DIANA-- GO!
?

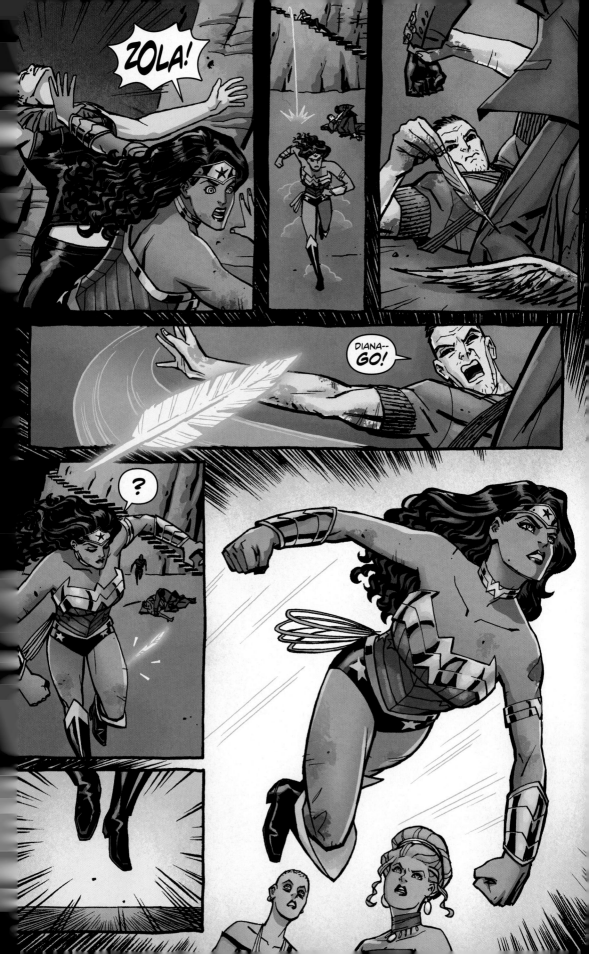

WONDER WOMAN!
HOW MANY TIMES DO I HAVE TO TELL YOU TO STAY CLOSE?

I HOPE WE CAN PUT THIS BEHIND US, MESSENGER...

THAT YOU'LL ADMIT IT WAS AN ERROR IN JUDGMENT AND YOU'RE READY TO SERVE...

...YOUR NEW KING.

KA-KOO KA-KOO

YES!

NEW KING?! HA! YOUR REIGN IS OVER BEFORE IT BEGINS!

RRRUMMBBLLLE

CAN'T YOU FEEL IT--? YOU'D DO WELL TO GET ON YOUR KNEES! THE ONLY KING OF HEAVEN--

"--ZEUS HAS RETURNED!"

THIS DOESN'T LOOK GOOD...

UHHHH!

HOW THE HELL AM I S'POSED TO LOOK? I'M HAVING A BABY!

I'M NOT LOOKING AT YOU, ZOLA...

PUSH.

"REALLY? THE ONLY KING, HERA...?"

PERHAPS I'VE MADE A GRAVE MISTAKE.
INDEED, APOLLO. ONE THAT WILL BURY YOU IN YOURS!
OR...
YOU IN YOUR GRAVE, HERA?
SEE, YOU'VE MISTAKEN THE AWE OF THE OLD...
"FOR THE SHOCK OF THE NEW.
"I AM KING. AND OLYMPUS--MY OLYMPUS--WILL NOW REFLECT THAT."
WHAT WAS IT YOU SAID ABOUT KNEES, HERA?
MY QUEEN... YOU'VE SHOWN YOUR TRUE COLORS.
PITY THEY'RE SO DARK...

...MY EXILED QUEEN.
SO, THEN, THE NEW KING IS A TYRANT?
IF NEED BE, TO PROTECT THIS FAMILY, I WILL BE.
EVEN IF IT MEANS SPLITTING IT APART?
AMAZON. BACK TO FULFILL YOUR PROMISE?
IF NEED BE.
APOLLO, I UNDERSTAND YOU'RE DRIVEN BY A PROPHECY AND ALL...
I MEAN, AS WE'VE JUST SEEN, WHO IN THIS FAMILY ISN'T?
BUT IN YOUR MAD GRAB FOR POWER, HAVE YOU STOPPED TO REALLY CONSIDER THAT IT'S ZOLA'S CHILD WHO WILL MURDER ONE OF YOU AND TAKE THE THRONE?

STRIFE!

SORRY. REALLY, I AM. BUT I CAN'T HELP MYSELF.

I MEAN, WHAT'S OBVIOUS, IF NOT THAT?

TA TA.

UUGH!

DIANA...

AGREED, HERMES--I THINK IT'S BEST TO GET ZOLA AWAY FROM HERE.

DO YOU TRUST ME?

...OF COURSE I DO.

CAN'T WAIT TO KISS THE BABY.

NOW, WHERE WERE WE?

THE PROMISE.

THAT YOU'D BEST ME.

HA!

REALLY? YOU STRIP YOURSELF OF YOUR BEST DEFENSE--

AGAINST A GOD?

MY DEFENSE?

MY CUFFS WERE YOURS.

ENOUGH!

I'VE MADE ONE DEAL THIS DAY. PERHAPS WE CAN MAKE ANOTHER...
SISTER?
A DEAL? HOW'S THIS...PROMISE THAT YOU WON'T COME AFTER THE BABY...
OR AS ZEUS' DAUGHTER, I'LL PERSONALLY FULFILL YOUR PROPHECY.
AGREED.
ON THE CONDITION THAT IF THE CHILD IS THE ONE WHO WILL SLAY A GOD TO TAKE A THRONE...

"...YOU WILL SLAY *IT*."

PUSH, ZOLA, PUSH...

"YOU'RE ALMOST THERE..."

BLACKBURN MEDICAL CENTER

?

BEEN LIKE THAT SINCE SHE GOT HERE.

APOLLO EXILED HER.

TAKEN OUR FATHER'S PLACE, THEN?

TAKEN AND MADE IT HIS OWN, LENNOX.

YOU LET 'IM?

IT DIDN'T SEEM IMPORTANT.

WHERE'S ZOLA?

HAVEN'T SEEN HER... SHOULD I 'AVE?

UH HUH
UH HUH... THAT WAS...

CAN I SEE MY BABY?

HERMES?

HERMES!!!!

ZOLA--
WHAT?

HE TOOK MY BABY! HERMES TOOK MY BABY!!!

WHAT ELSE WOULD YOU *EXPECT* FROM THE GOD OF THIEVES?

WHERE IS HE?!!

AAAH!

YOU *INSOLENT* LITTLE *WHORE!* I'LL--

HERA... YOU'RE--

BLEEDING? THAT'S IMPOSSIBLE... I'M--

MORTAL, I'D SAY.

ZOLA--LISTEN-- I SWEAR ON MY OWN *LIFE* THAT I WILL FIND YOUR CHILD AND BRING IT BACK TO YOU!

I WILL NOT REST, MY DEAR FRIEND--WE ARE BOTH BETRAYED THIS DAY. I WILL FIND HERMES...
I WILL HUNT HIM TIRELESSLY. I WILL FIND YOUR BABY...
"AND I WILL MAKE HERMES PAY FOR WHAT HE'S STOLEN FROM YOU."
WAAA!
CRYING? HEH.
I THINK IT MAY BE A BIT EARLY FOR THAT.
A BABY CAN'T HELP BUT DO THAT, THIEF.
THIS CHILD, DEMETER? IT WILL HAVE PLENTY TO CRY ABOUT LATER.

"BETRAYAL, DEATH...
"PERHAPS THE FALL OF OLYMPUS.
"OR DEPENDING HOW YOU LOOK AT IT...
"A BEGINNING.
"NEW GODS."
BOOM
END

Wonder Woman's divine armor

Hephaestus

Artemis

Eros

Demeter

WONDER WOMAN #7 cover sketches

WONDER
WOMAN

WONDER
WOMAN

WONDER
WOMAN

"If you liked The Dark Knight, THE JOKER is a must-have for your bookshelf."
—MTV.com

"A deeply disturbing and completely unnerving work, a literary achievement that takes its place right alongside Alan Moore's THE KILLING JOKE."
—IGN.com

FROM THE EISNER AWARD-WINNING WRITER OF *100 BULLETS*
BRIAN AZZARELLO
with LEE BERMEJO

LUTHOR

with LEE BERMEJO

SUPERMAN: FOR TOMORROW

with JIM LEE

BATMAN: BROKEN CITY

with EDUARDO RISSO

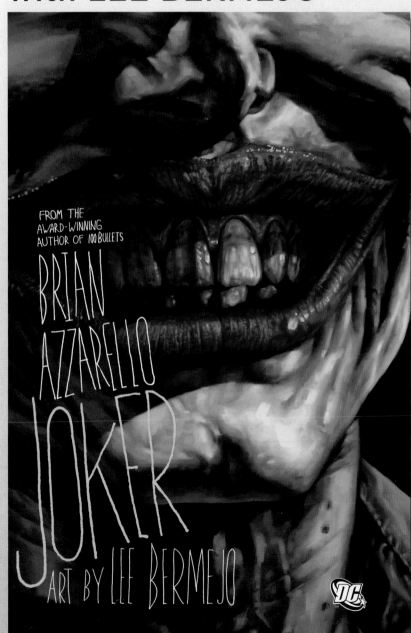

"Clear storytelling at its best. It's an intriguing concept and easy to grasp."
—NEW YORK TIMES

"Azzarello is rebuilding the mythology of Wonder Woman."
–MAXIM

START AT THE BEGINNING!

WONDER WOMAN VOLUME 1: BLOOD

MR. TERRIFIC
VOLUME 1:
MIND GAMES

BLUE BEETLE
VOLUME 1:
METAMORPHOSIS

THE FURY OF FIRESTORM:
THE NUCLEAR MEN
VOLUME 1:
GOD PARTICLE

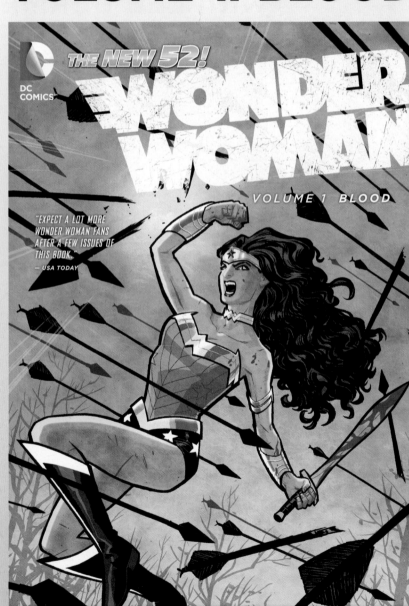